## REFLECTION JOURNAL

# İGNITE
### —YOUR—
# SUPER
# SIGHT

**THE POWER OF SPIRITUAL VISION TO FUEL
YOUR FUTURE AND MOVE MOUNTAINS**

# JULIA KITZ

First Edition, September 2023

ISBN: 979-8-9886603-2-3

Vision 2 Victory

Cincinnati, Ohio, U.S.A.

vision2victory.org

# Contents

# Introduction

## REFLECTION QUESTIONS

*These reflection questions are designed to correspond with the book **Ignite Your Super Sight: The Power of Spiritual Vision to Fuel Your Future and Move Mountains** by Julia Kitz.*

- Have you ever felt like a phony or an imposter Christian? In which ways?

- Which areas of your Christian walk could use an improvement or a little boost?

- Have you ever believed that you could do something great for God? Why or why not?

# CHAPTER 1
# THE DIVINE FILTER

**REFLECTION QUESTIONS**

- Think of any negative, challenging, or unfruitful things that are preventing you from living the abundant life Jesus promised. These are your "mountains" so to speak. List anything that you consider to be a "mountain" that is standing in your way:

- On a scale of one to ten, rank how well-developed you think you are in the following areas: Faith (Believing God and what He says) _____ /10; Speech (Speaking in agreement with God) _____ /10; and Spiritual Vision (Seeing your future as God intends) _____ /10.

- Have you ever had what you would consider a "supernatural experience"? How did it change you or your relationship with God?

- What are some things are you hungry for, or seeking more of, regarding the Holy Spirit?

- In which ways do you think God speaks to you?

# CHAPTER 2
# THE EIGHT ELEMENTS OF SPIRITUAL VISION

## REFLECTION QUESTIONS

As a starting point, how well can you answer the following questions during this season of your life?

- What am I here for and what has God planned for my life?

- Which direction is my life taking and is it part of God's plan?

- How can I feel closer to God and sense the leading of the Holy Spirit?

- Where can I find more energy and joy in my life?

- How can I view my circumstances and challenges differently?

- Where will I find the strength and ability to do what God asks of me?

- How will God meet my needs abundantly?

- How can I find more contentment and satisfaction in my life?

Now go back and circle or highlight the questions you had a difficult time answering. Those are the areas you might want to focus on as you discover the eight elements of spiritual vision throughout the book.

# CHAPTER 3
# THE SECRETS OF THE SEERS

**REFLECTION QUESTIONS**

- In this chapter, you discovered the secrets of the ancient biblical seers. Which one(s) can you relate to the most and why?

- How has God "shown" you things or "spoken" to you in the past?

- In what other ways do you think God would like to communicate with you?

- Reread Joel 2:28 and Acts 2:17. What stands out to you in those verses?

# CHAPTER 4

# ILLUMINATING THE WAY

## REFLECTION QUESTIONS

- What do you think are some of the unique purposes God has for your life?

- Are there any divine assignments that you believe the Holy Spirit has given you?

- How might you become a more authentic Christian?  What would that look like?

# CHAPTER 5

# IN STEP WITH THE SPIRIT

## REFLECTION QUESTIONS

- What kind of "season" do you find yourself in currently?

- How can you take the next step at this moment with Jesus?

- Are there any situations, circumstances, or places in your life that God might be using to prepare you for greater things in the future?

- Which areas of your life might you be trying to steer that the Holy Spirit would like to lead?

# Chapter 6

# DIVINE INDWELLING

**REFLECTION QUESTIONS**

- When do you seem to sense God's presence the most?

- How can you increase those types of experiences in your schedule?

- If you could spend an afternoon with the Lord, where would you go and what would you do with Him? Close your eyes and imagine the scene. Describe it:

# Chapter 7

# PURE PASSION

## REFLECTION QUESTIONS

- Which things in your life have you been doing *without* passion or purpose?

- How might those things change if God's love was the motivation behind it?

- In what meaningful ways could you put God's love into action?

# CHAPTER 8
# THE VIEW FROM ABOVE

## REFLECTION QUESTIONS

- Which giftings and talents do you have that can benefit others?

- Which activities and endeavors in your life have been divinely prompted and completed with God's help?

- How have you had to collaborate with other individuals in fulfilling divine assignments?

- In what areas do you need to shift your focus from an earthly perspective to a heavenly one?

# CHAPTER 9
# EMPOWERED FOR MORE

**REFLECTION QUESTIONS**

- What has God's amazing grace empowered you to do?

- What do you still want to do that will require a measure of God's supernatural grace?

- How have you allowed the enemy to stifle your effectiveness through fear and unbelief?

# CHAPTER 10
## ENVISION THE PROVISION

**REFLECTION QUESTIONS**

- Close your eyes and envision a spiritual basket, full of provision, on the table in front of you. What's inside of it?

- How has the Holy Spirit imparted wisdom and guidance to you in the past?

- What do you need God's wisdom for now?

## Chapter 11
## Peace From Another Place

**REFLECTION QUESTIONS**

- What does the biblical definition of peace (shared in this chapter) mean to you?

- How can you prioritize and protect the divine rest of God in the upcoming days or weeks?

- What are some activities and endeavors that bring you a feeling of peace?

# CHAPTER 12
# VARYING VIEWPOINTS

## REFLECTION QUESTIONS

- Which of the common optical conditions from this chapter might be limiting your *spiritual* vision?

- In which ways would you like the Holy Spirit to correct your spiritual eyes of misunderstanding?

# CHAPTER 13
# TWELVE KEYS THAT UNLOCK SPIRITUAL VISION

## REFLECTION QUESTIONS

*These questions accompany the Activation Activities for each of the twelve keys listed in Chapter 13.*

## KEY #1

Study the three accounts of the Parable of the Sower in the Gospels: Matthew 13:1-23; Mark 4:1-34; and Luke 8:4-18. Reflect and pray about the following:

- In which phase of farming the seed of God's Word into your heart do you find yourself?

- Are there any parts of the Bible that you are struggling to believe for yourself?

- How have difficult circumstances and situations kept you from staying in God's Word?

- What do you think may be distracting you from spending time reading the Bible?

- How could you set aside some time soon to plant more of God's Word into your heart?

## KEY #2

- How has the Holy Spirit been leading you in certain circumstances or conversations over the past few weeks?

- Read Isaiah 43:19. What new things do you think God wants to do in your life?

## KEY #3

- Meditate on several of the scriptures listed in the Appendix at the end of the book. Write down 3 of your favorites:

- What may God be revealing to you with these scriptures?

# KEY #4

- Which of the visionary verses and scriptures stand out to you as you read them aloud?

- What do you believe God can do for you right now? Write your ideas down and declare them out loud in faith.

# KEY #5

- Write out your prayer (as guided in the activation activity) here:

## KEY #6

Write down any thoughts, impressions, images, or words you heard during the worship activation activity:

## KEY #7

- What are your thoughts about journaling? Has it ever been productive for you? Why or why not?

- Try to remember some of the wonderful things that the Lord has done for you! Record a few here:

## KEY #8

- Which goals, dreams, and desires have you envisioned for yourself or your family in the past?


- Which encouraging words have others spoken to you regarding your future?


- What did you enjoy doing when you were young?


- What do you think God created you to do or to be?


- Can you recall any significant answered prayers? Record a few here:


- Which step of faith do you believe God wants you to take toward a particular vision or goal?


- How might God be preparing you for the next phase or season to come?

- What did God say to you (could be an inner voice or a prompting) a while back that you may have ignored or forgotten?

## KEY #9

- How do you see yourself?

- How do you regard your family?

- How do you consider your community?

- How do you view your role at church?

- How do you regard others?

- How do you perceive God?

- Where do you see God working in your life?


- Do you notice any patterns in your perspective or any misleading filters?


## KEY #10

- What are some things that give you a sense of **purpose** or accomplishment?


- In which direction would you like to see your life go and where is God **positioning** you?


- When do you feel the closest to God or sense His **presence** the most?


- Which types of activities energize and motivate you or fill you with **passion**?


- When are you most focused on maintaining an eternal and heavenly **perspective?**

- When have you really felt God's supernatural **power** at work in you?

- Where have you seen God's **provision** in your life when you needed it most?

- What causes you to feel most grounded and at **peace**?

# KEY #11

- What may God be unveiling and revealing to you regarding your spiritual eyesight?

- What are you able to see with your eyes of faith now?

- What do you want to see in your future?

- Which ideas and concepts might you include in your vision board?

# KEY #12

- Which outcomes, results, or impact do you want to achieve?

- How will God change and develop you through these outcomes?

- What might God want to create or accomplish through you?

- Who might God want to help through you?

- How do you think God will help you manage to do this?

- What would God's perfect future for yourself and your family look like?

- What do you think God's vision is for your life right now?

- My vision statement:

## SPIRITUAL VISION CHECKLIST

Use this checklist to help determine how many of the eight elements of spiritual vision are found in your pursuits and/or endeavors.

# SPIRITUAL VISION CHECKLIST

## EIGHT ELEMENTS OF GOD-GIVEN VISION:

- ⚬ Authenticate your PURPOSE.
- ⚬ Direct your POSITION.
- ⚬ Encourage God's PRESENCE.
- ⚬ Ignite your PASSION.
- ⚬ Apply eternal PERSPECTIVE.
- ⚬ Include Holy Spirit POWER.
- ⚬ Require divine PROVISION.
- ⚬ Bring supernatural PEACE.